MOVED BY A MUSTARD SEED
~THE POWER OF FAITH~

Lisa Miller-Baldwin

Copyright© 2013 by Lisa Baldwin Publishing

Email: lisamillerbaldwin@yahoo.com

Design Cover by: Paula McDade, Angel Unaware

Unless otherwise indicated, all Scripture quotations are taken from the Holy Bible:

New International Version and King James Version. NIV. Used by permission of Zondervan Publishing House.

Lisa Baldwin Publishing has made every effort to trace the ownership of all quotes. In the event of a question arising from the use of a poem or quote, we regret any error made and will be pleased to make the necessary correction in future editions of this book.

All rights reserved. No part of this publication may be reproduced in any form or by any form or by any electronic or mechanical means, including information storage and retrieval system without permission in writing from the publisher, expect by a reviewer who may quote brief passages in a review.

Printed in the United States of America
ISBN: 978-0615785509

This BOOK IS DEDICATED TO:

My five beautiful children: Clarence III, Marquise, Elizabeth, Kentrell, and my youngest Me'lisa. If you receive half the joy you have given me, you'll radiate the rest of your life. My prayer is that you take this book to heart realizing you can MOVE mountains if you place your trust in God.

Table of Contents

Acknowledgements 1

Introduction 2

Move Your Mountain With Your Mouth 3

The Mustard Seed Trail 6

Are You Feeding Your Faith? 11

My Faith Confessions 16

My Journey.....My Provision 18

Build Your Faith 31

God Wants Me To Do What? 34

No Matter What! 39

Conclusion 44

Acknowledgements

A word to some special people who brought much encouragement and support that aided in the completion of this book.

To my supportive husband, mother, sister and brother thanks for believing in the "Impossible". You made my life's journey very interesting and exciting!

Sarah Smith—Thanks for always being my #1 cheerleader. You consistently encouraged me to always commit to what God has called me to do. Even when others doubted, you were my saving grace.

Dawniel Winningham—Thanks for pushing me and being the fuel to ignite my fire! I yet remember your words. FINISH YOUR BOOK! Thank you!

Paula McDade—You are definitely my angel, your company Angel Unaware is so befitting! Thank you for giving the design of the book that will bring many to pick up and be blessed.

Aprille-Franks-Hunt---I greatly appreciate you sharing your expertise and encouraging me to put my pen where my mouth was. Thank you!

And especially the Giver of all words: I thank you for allowing this dream to manifest. Please allow the words of this book to minister and compel the ones that read it, that the best of life is found while believing and trusting in YOU.

Introduction

Faith... The size of a mustard seed, All things are possible!

Faith is believing in something when common sense tells you not to.
(Miracle On The 34th Street)

The journey that I began to fulfill my life's purpose has been a story made for television. Each scene was filled with many instances of God's faithfulness and his discipline. In spite of my numerous mistakes God created something beautiful and worthy of an Oscar. I must note the mistakes that I made ONLY occurred when I trusted in Lisa, relationships, income, and the source of many problems, "PEOPLE". The script continues to unfold and bear witness that if you allow the "Mustard Seed" to move. All things are possible!

Moved By A Mustard Seed~The Power Of Faith

Move Your Mountain With Your Mouth

Never talk defeat. Use words like hope, belief, faith, victory
Norman Vincent-Peale

I am totally convinced that you have the ability to shape your future with YOUR words. Are you ready to open that business, further your education, buy your dream home, or patent that unique invention? SPEAK IT! Let's declare today the things that you desire tomorrow. If you have mountains in your life you want removed, SPEAK TO IT! Words are powerful and have lasting effects. Active faith is orally spoken, because faith has a voice. Faith communicates what faith believes. Forcefully speaking to circumstances makes them change; that is how God changed things He did not want, into what He wanted them to become. We are made in His image, so that we can change mountain problems to answers.

Believing and speaking God's promise makes circumstances obey you, because you believe and not doubt. What is a **MOUNTAIN** in a believer's life? The mountain is the **PROBLEM** in your life. The mountain is anything that is adverse or contrary to the **Word of God** for your life. A mountain is anything that is a barrier to you completing God's Will. A mountain is anything that is slowing down or impeding your progress in the Kingdom of God.

Many believers spend time **praying** to God about their mountain. They describe the mountain in full detail to God. They inform God of the exact dimensions of the mountain. They cry and moan to God about what a hindrance or impossibility the mountain is in their life.

Jesus didn't tell us to **IGNORE** or **DENY** the mountain or problem. We are not to say, "I don't have a mountain" or "what problem?" We are not to practice **positive thinking** and say over and over; "I can climb over that mountain, I will go around that mountain, it want stop me". A positive attitude is always good. But a positive attitude is not what Jesus said to do with mountains. Jesus said to **speak** to the mountain or problem and tell it to be moved

Authority is exhibited by speaking. You speak to persons or things that you have authority over. You don't ask or plead; you direct and require. You exhibit faith when you speak to things instead of asking God to speak for you. When you speak instead of asking, you demonstrate an understanding of God's Word. You can't walk with God unless you agree with His Word. Faith involves you placing confidence in God's word and responding to it. The God-like faith will demonstrate itself by speaking and trusting in God's provision.

The Mustard Seed Trail

"YOU WILL REAP WHAT YOU SOW."

"Be not deceived; God is not mocked: for whatsoever a man soweth, that shall he also reap." (Galatians 6:7 KJV)

Life is realized in the smallest of beginnings. In the human body growth is directed by DNA- proteins wound in a double-stranded helix, which is composed of amino acids, which are composed of molecules so small no microscope could bring them into view. Considering this, should it surprise us that a tree could emerge from the germination of a tiny mustard seed. Our limitations are drawn by the boundaries we build around ourselves. Those boundaries are composed from awareness of our humanity -- our blemished imperfection, our fear of failure which causes a fight for stepping out into the unknown or remaining in what's comfortable.

While we live in our shadow of imperfection, the world moves and breathes around us as molecules collide forming the backbone of creation. The beauty of the parable of the mustard seed is the portrayal of life -- the vision of strength and protection that emerges from the seed of an insignificant mustard seed.

It is amazing how God can use us in spite of obvious inadequacies if we make ourselves available to be used. Only in the hands of our Creator can our full potential be realized. Despite our imperfection, weaknesses, and faults, God can bring from our efforts a great harvest. He can bring out of our insecurity and insignificance a tree that will shelter the heads of those around us, which will provide a sanctuary of stability and support.

One, mustard seed grows every place in the world...in cold climates as well as hot ones. It can grow in any type of soil. It is a hardy seed.

Seed growth depends on both internal and external conditions. The most important external factors include temperature, water, oxygen and sometimes light or darkness.

So this brings us to a very important question. What are you planting and under what conditions are you planting? Your mustard seed will NOT grow if it isn't planted in the right soil receiving the proper nutrients to thrive and survive!

Take this time to jot down barriers or hindrances that have hindered your mustard seed (FAITH) to grow.

_____

_____

_____

_____

_____

_____

_____

_____

_____

_____

_____

_____

_____

_____

Now let's create FAITH affirmations to grow on:

Example: My Faith moves mountains every single day. God has Faith in me to carry through on the passion that He placed in my heart.

_____

_____

_____

_____

_____

_____

_____

_____

_____

_____

_____

_____

Are You Feeding Your Faith?

"I cannot remember every book I've read any more than the meals I have eaten; even so, they have made me."
— Ralph Waldo Emerson

Faith grows as you feed your faith. Will it grow, hibernate or remain dormant? Let's take a look at a dormant seed and a seed in hibernation. Both are NOT fulfilling its purpose because of the lack of exercise. We are truly a product of what we eat or feed ourselves.

If you establish an environment of faith, you will say what you want to come to pass and you will have what you say.

Here are some things you may not know about a mustard seed. A mustard seed is very resilient. It is totally unaffected by its surroundings. No matter what is happening in the garden the mustard seed stays true to itself continuing to grow. If you plant it in your garden it will take over the place. Let's take a look at two definitions that faith builders should avoid.

1. Seed **dormancy**: means the seed does not develop for a while *even when conditions are suitable*.
2. Seed **hibernation**: fails to grow because conditions are not right. Growth is triggered by particular events in the environment.

So, it is very important to remain in environments that will promote and propel growth. If a plant is never given proper water or sunshine it will die! The same holds true regarding your faith, if it isn't watered and placed in the correct environment. Faith will die!

Let's look at factors that contribute to growth and success:

Surrounding yourself with positive individuals and those that propel and encourage the impossible. When Jesus arrived at the house of Jairus, he did not let anyone go in with him except Peter, John and James, and the child's father and mother. Why? These individuals had FAITH in the impossible and trusted for the best. You must realize everyone will not embrace the impossible but take ONLY those who believe and celebrate the ability of a loving and faithful God. Sometimes we must travel with the minority to receive an abundant blessing. There will ALWAYS be those who ridicule and laugh at what looks to be unachievable but let your spirit and faith lead the way to your miracle. God always has the last laugh. Ask Sarah. Let's delve deeper in Luke 8:51-56. 52 Meanwhile, all the people were wailing and mourning for her. "Stop wailing," Jesus said. "She is not dead but asleep." They laughed at him, knowing that she was dead. 54 But he took her by the hand and said, "My child, get up!" Her spirit returned, and at once she stood up.

What barriers or situations are you allowing to cause disbelief?

_____

_____

_____

_____

_____

_____

_____

_____

_____

_____

_____

_____

You must deal with your unbelief. You must remove the scoffers and the unbelievers as Jesus did. You must establish an environment of faith by removing the interior and exterior unbelief. We must grasp and apply to our heart and spirit what Jesus said to those who doubted. "Don't be afraid; just believe." Only unbelief will stop you from doing the supernatural. You must deal with any area of unbelief by increasing your time with God in prayer. You must also fast or decrease your dependency on your flesh, worldly input, and sensory input. To increase your faith take the lead of the mustard seed.

Little is much when it comes from God. The mustard seed in the parable grows to be a huge tree, representing the tiny beginnings.

So, too, does the tiniest bit of faith, when it is true faith from God, grow to immense proportions in the lives of believers and spreading out to influence all they come into contact with. One has only to read histories of the great men of the faith, to know that superhuman feats were performed by those whose faith was, at one time, only the size of a mustard seed.

My Faith Confessions

Blessed is the man who trusts in the Lord and has made the Lord his hope and confidence. – Jeremiah 17:7

1. I believe the **whosoever clause** of John 3:16 and the "**whosoever clause**" of Mark 11:23.

2. I am a "whosoever", so I can **speak** to the mountain (problem/barrier to my receiving or doing God's Will for my life) and tell it to be removed and be cast in the sea [some dimension that I do not occupy].

3. I **say** what I want to "come to pass" by the Word of God. I will **ONLY** say what I want to "come to pass", to become, to come into existence, or begin to be.

4. I will not be **DIVIDED** in my mind. I will not go from confidence in the Word of God to no confidence. I will not be like a wave in the sea going back and forth in my mind. I realize according to James 1:6, that I will not receive anything from God if I am wavering.

5. I will eliminate doubt by renewing my mind according to the Word of God [Romans 12:2].

Faith involves you placing confidence in God's spoken word and responding to it. The God-like faith will demonstrate itself by speaking and trusting the spoken word of God.

I can say to any non-fruitful thing that I encounter in my life, "Let no fruit grow on you ever again, because I do the same works that Jesus did [Matthew 21:19, Mark 11:14, John 14:12].

I will not pray and ask God to do for me, what I have the authority and ability to do for myself.

I use my authority by "speaking" to any barrier that is stopping God's will [Luke 10:19].

My Journey…..My Provision

You don't have to see the whole staircase. Just take the first step.
Martin Luther King, Jr.

I stepped out into a journey of the unknown with a mandate by God to fulfill his call on my life. I felt ill equipped for such a daunting task. Oh what a journey my life has taken, filled with twists and turns and unexpected miracles. Let me share with you my story. I grew up in an abusive volatile home. My dad was in our life that is, my sister and my brother sporadically. One week he was there, the next two weeks was a possibility that is, if he wasn't on one of his drinking binges. My father was an alcoholic who beat my mother relentlessly, I am now

46 years old and the image of my mother underneath the kitchen table sobbing and begging for the blows to cease just hasn't escaped my memory.

My father stole money or anything of value from our home to support his addiction. He even stole my opportunity to have a DAD. Every little girl dreams of being cared for and adored by her father. All I could do was envy children who had their father's presence emotionally and physically. I sought for affirmation from my father by making good grades. Needless to say, the only praise that I received was from my mother. Thank God for mothers who attempt to fill two roles, and still maintain their sanity. So with the lack of love, attention and affirmation I went searching for something, something I yearned for, a "father". Ironically I did not just find a father. I found my father. After high-school I married who I thought would be my savior, my redeemer of all I had experienced,(my mistake) I just knew this man would protect me, support me, love me, and cherish me. So I thought. Needless to say the same behaviors that my father displayed, my husband repeated. He invoked fear and humiliation. He was cruel and mean with his words.

I never realized how powerful and penetrating words were, and how they lingered in your mind and spirit. I begin to live in a prison I couldn't seem to break free from. I wanted to escape the hellhole I lived in. But what would I do? Where would I go? What would people say? And the most agonizing question, What about my children? I had ironclad excuses to continue to subject myself and my children to such undeserved cruelty. I had five children who needed their father.

I also had a reverential respect for marriage, and despised the idea of being alone! These reasons kept me behind prison walls year after year. But all along God was preparing me for something much greater than myself. Because of the abuse, I was an empty young lady. I sought love and affirmation in all the wrong places. I begin to allow relationships to define who I was. I began to shop to fill the empty places in my heart.

Needless to say I looked beautiful on the outside but felt terrible on the inside.

Not realizing God could only fill the void of a woman wanting to be loved. After many years attempting to find love! I found love and affirmation in Christ. It happened one morning during my devotional time with God, he took me to a passage that has changed my life. (Psalms 139:14 KJV) I will praise thee for I am FEARFULLY and WONDERFULLY MADE. After I read this passage and accepted its truth into my heart. A metamorphosis took place. I released the selfish attitude that it was all about me, and took on the attitude that THROUGH Christ I can do ALL things! God later told me," You become the answer to someone else's prayer and share my love, concern and grace as I have shown you! I obeyed, and then founded the Wonderfully Made Foundation. The Wonderfully Made Foundation is a non-profit 501 c 3 organization serving families that are homeless with housing and housing services including, case management, transportation, classes of enrichment, and goal setting. The organization also provides clothing to the less-fortunate, and prides itself in its newest program, Wonderfully Made Foundation Family Literacy program. The organization was initially founded for victims or potential victims of domestic violence that felt alone, empty, unloved, and not valuable. But God expanded our services with very little including money and resources. God allowed the organization to touch over 3,000 Oklahomans with our domestic violence awareness events. It didn't stop there I put to paper my journey through domestic violence and wrote a stage play entitled, Mirror, Mirror On The Wall. What an empowering experience, that became my saving grace as well as many others that were touched by this production. I possessed little to no money and lacked resources and equipment. But guess what? God PROVIDED!! The production was heralded, A MUST SEE! He took the tiny little mustard seed in my hand and made something BIG! The production was later translated to Spanish entitled, Espejito, Espejito. This production made history it was the FIRST ever Hispanic production in my state. Even in the midst of the naysayers, and the critics I yet moved my faith! Yes I moved pass what others thought and focused on what God thought. I was ridiculed because I don't speak Spanish. SO WHAT!! God uses individuals who rely on him, not themselves. Guess what? He PROVIDED! But his provision didn't stop there. He continued to show himself strong. We needed an office to begin the assignment. So I scheduled a meeting with my Pastor at the time, and shared our need and desire to begin the ministry at the church. My Pastor LOVED the mission and heart of the Wonderfully Made Foundation. So he graciously allowed us to office at the church and provided seed money for the organization to begin its mission. Isn't God good! A short while later God expanded the organization's mission to not only provide domestic violence awareness to the community but to begin offering services to the homeless, single parents, referral agency for food, clothing, counseling , and drug and alcohol addiction assistance. The odd thing about God is that when he gives you a mandate each step is not totally absolute. But with the tiny mustard seed in your hand it qualifies everything ABSOLUTE! So I then continued to follow God's lead. Due to the numerous calls from women with children that were homeless. I advocated for a vacant property that my family owned to become the new home of the Wonderfully Made Foundation Homeless Home. On August 1, 2011 we began to house homeless families providing them with hope, housing and a better tomorrow. This task was and IS not easy. I was not rich in money, but very rich in love. But LOVE doesn't pay the bills. So this God-ordered task became VERY scary. How was I going to pay the bills? Only my mustard seed could answer that question. Every time a need arose God provided. I kept the homeless home afloat with my personal income and God's favor. I took God at his word, and yet pushed on, in the midst of my tears and fears. So, after leaving the church where we had our office, the organization needed the 501c 3 umbrella that was previously provided with our affiliation with the church. This documentation allows donations received to become tax-deductible which is a great incentive for most to give. Within one week of leaving our previous office. A very giving person donated to the Wonderfully Made Foundation a 501 c 3. This documentation usually costs anywhere from $1,000-3,000.00. But with the mustard yet in my hand DID NOT cost us one red cent. The many doors that was opened and created caused the mustard seed in my hand to grow bigger. But the challenges and obstacles also grew. I can vividly recall a personal bill that had to be paid. Unfortunately, I was unable to do so because it would prevent the utilities at the homeless shelter from getting paid. But, then.........God intervened. An individual came by the homeless shelter and handed me a bank envelope with $700.00 enclosed! Wow!!

It met the need and revealed to me the scripture, that states when you give to the poor you lend to God. But did God stop there? NO!! As bills came in that I could not meet, God did! I was sitting in a church service and following the service a woman who I did not know approaches me and gives me a check for $500.00. I cried, I shouted and I thanked God for again coming through. His provision is amazing and true. To again illustrate how God will move for you if you totally believe and rely on his ability to provide. Let me share another provision moment . The organization needed a website which would be costly. I did not possess any monies for this expense and realized the significance of a business making its presence known on-line. God showed up again, Richard Osei with ROIT Consulting a local website and graphic business generously donated the Wonderfully Made Foundation its website and my personal website with management at NO COST! The costs of these websites, particularly the caliber of creation would have exceeded $8,000.00 in fees for both. I stepped out into the unknown with the vision of the Wonderfully Made Foundation not knowing when and how provision would occur but God NEVER disappointed me, or abandoned me. As of this writing, the Wonderfully Made Foundation was selected as a finalist by the Oklahoma Center for Non-Profits Excellence Award. Out of 19,000 non-profits in our state 24 were selected and praise God Wonderfully Made Foundation was one of the 24 and will receive $5,000.00 which will aid in our operation expenses. This action and others shared and not shared occurred because of my TOTAL dependence on God and assurance that he will come through!! Even when I thought provision would come from other sources including sources that provide for the poor and needy, they didn't. I came to realize God is my ONLY source.

My dependence and trust was in HIM, not PEOPLE. When God calls you to complete a task, dream or assignment he will provide you with the tools and resources to be successful. But you mustn't give up!! Even in the face of uncertainties and lack! Work your FAITH just as God did for Moses. HE WILL DO FOR YOU! He will provide a ram in the bush. [13] Abraham looked up and there in a thicket he saw a ram caught by its horns. He went over and took the ram and sacrificed it as a burnt offering instead of his son. [14] So Abraham called that place The LORD Will Provide. And to this day it is said, "On the mountain of the LORD it will be provided." Genesis 22:13 NIV.

Yes, he provides for those who use the mustard seed in their hand which speaks volumes to our FATHER, that says I BELIEVE and place my trust in YOU not my circumstances. 2 Cor. 5:7 says that we must live by faith *NOT* by sight. Seeing can be very deceiving. Let's keep our eyes affixed and focused on God.

Faith is the key to success! You may not be rich, famous, or have the right political connections. But if you have God, that is ENOUGH! I saw God move for me and the Wonderfully Made Foundation without ANY of those things. I can recall a conversation with a lady that asked, "What do you do for marketing? A little embarrassed because I knew the budget didn't allow for this expense. I replied with the truth, outside of social media I don't. But shortly after that conversation another ram appeared when a couple of television stations contacted my office to interview me concerning our work in the community. So when money wasn't accessible God invented media exposure that again DID NOT cost our VERY strict budget. So my journey has been incredible and filled with many twists and turns but God has remained faithful. Even when discouragement and malicious attacks would come I yet kept focused on what God has commissioned me to do. I stay connected to his presence with prayer, devotions, bible study and worship! I worship God for who HE is and what I AM NOT.

No doubt you have heard the old example about having faith in a chair. Saying you trust the chair to support you is nothing more than words until that faith is exercised. It's when you actually sit and rest in it that faith is realized. That is how faith is proved out —it's only then that you can know that the chair is trustworthy.

As you journey through life, you can see faith do the same things that seeds do. They grow into something much bigger than what they started. Your faith —trust in God— will also grow and you will be amazed by what He does with you. Does that mean that if you trust God to change something (take away the bad and bring on the good circumstances), that it will happen? No, moving the mountain is about taking away the fearful thoughts so that the circumstances are no longer something to dread. It no longer holds power over you because you trust God to do what is good for you and those around you.

God took the Israelites through many journeys. Whenever there were difficult encounters, they saw Him at work. He took them across the sea and the river; He gave them food and drink; He drove out their enemies before them. They piled up stones as reminders of what He had done for them at these junctions. Remembering His faithfulness is like looking at the mustard seed to remind yourself that He is real –that He gives life its purpose.

Do not despise humble beginnings. Start small grow big; The journey of a thousand kilometers starts with the first step. Begin where you are and allow NOTHING to destroy your determination or purpose. The mustard seed is incorruptible, that is why it will grow and not decay or perish. The growth is slow but sure, and there is no end in sight about its growth.

A seed grows and so can faith. Faith that is not used will not grow; but if it is used, it increases. By our faith and commitment, we can be more Christ-like and witness to others about the faithfulness of God. Mustard seeds generally take three to ten days to germinate if placed under the proper conditions.

Build Your Faith

Faith is building on what you know is here so you can reach what you know is there

Cullen Hightower

Focus on building *your own* faith. The gift God gives you is enough, but you can build upon what you have. Romans 10:17 says that faith comes by hearing and hearing by the Word of God. God's Word is Truth; you build your faith by getting the truth into your heart. Not YOUR truth, not society's truth, but God's truth!

You can't read or hear the Word then put it on a bookshelf. What happens when you do that? Well, what happens when you quit exercising and eating too much? You gain weight and lose your muscle. What happens when you don't focus on giving in your marriage and focus on the getting part? The marriage suffers. What happens when you let you garden go? The weeds come in and overtake the plants. The same thing happens when you stay out of the Word. You forget what the Word says and how to apply it to situations in your life.

So by reading the Word of God is how you increase your faith. Keep in the Word, by reading, listening to tapes, listening to others teach and share until the Word is in your heart and you live, breathe, speak, walk and act on God's Word at all times. Keep a close fellowship with God. Keep combining your faith with the faith of others. Keep *doing* what God tells you that you can do!

"Have faith in God." This is where it all begins. The words I want you to focus on here are, do not doubt, and believe what God says, ask and believe you receive. So when you pray you need to say the Word, talk the Word and act on the Word. Hebrew 11:6 says that without faith it is impossible to please God, because everyone who comes to Him must believe.

Yes, faith is a very powerful tool, yet so few really use it. This is how powerful Hebrews 11:1 says it is: *"Now faith is the assurance of things hoped for, the conviction of things not seen."* The King James Version says, *"Now faith is the substance of things hoped for, the evidence of things unseen."* This means that what you hope for has substance or is a reality because of your faith and faith is the evidence that what you hoped for is a reality.

Recognize that you have faith and that you can cause it to grow. Feed your faith and exercise it right where you are in your Christian walk. Then your faith can grow and

God Wants Me To Do What?

Faith, doesn't make things easy, it makes things possible
Luke 1:37

I have learned that my problems, which I call challenges, will either **stop** me, **stress** me or **stretch** me according to the size of my thinking and faith. Each time that I've been stretched to grow beyond my comfort zone, God was there. Each time I was stretched; I tapped into my power of creative problem solving, my flexibility, my sense of humor, my intelligence, my ability to let go, my inner strength and yes, stretched to give, be and do more than I ever knew was possible. Once you've been stretched to a new level of faith, vision and endurance --- you can't go back to old thinking. Stretching your faith and using your mental muscles to move mountains will allow you to be the head and not the tail of your circumstances. I learned this very lesson when God instructed me to host a Christian conference, entitled the Entrepreneur of Faith Conference~Doing Business God's Way. I didn't feel comfortable in doing such a huge task without monies to host the event in excellence. The beauty of faith is that you don't have to have all the answers, but just a word from God. So I took my mustard seed and began to plan and implement steps to make this conference happen. Within 2 weeks of making the announcement of the upcoming conference, a caterer contacted me and offered her services at NO COST! If you know anything about events catering and the rental of a venue are the largest expenses. So God has already eliminated one of my worries. Again it didn't stop there. I begin to look for a venue that would accommodate the conference. But as both you and I know, venues aren't FREE! Yes, they are if YOU have a mustard seed clutched in your hand. I obtained a state-of the art venue that when seen, mouths were dropped! I can't blame them, because mine dropped as well. God had already taken care of my hugest concerns and my inability to provide the best. Miracle by miracle was provided putting God's stamp of approval on a perceived mountain. Just when I thought he was finished he provided the ultimate and most sought after keynote speaker for this conference. After the announcement revealing who our keynote speaker was, people again were flabbergasted and consistently inquired, how did you get him? My reply, "GOD"! By the way the keynote speaker was Mr. David Green, billionaire and Founder/CEO of Hobby Lobby Stores, Inc. heralding over 500 stores nationwide. I am so glad that I stepped out of my comfort zone and relied on God's tugging and his faithfulness to provide for what he had purposed. God calls us to depend on Him, so He rarely tells us about 10 steps down His path for us. He calls us to take that first step and trust Him with the rest. Don't get hung up on the possibility of missing "God's very best." Don't get caught in the American consumerism trap of playing the options, waiting for something that might be a bit better. Don't get stuck waiting for God to show you all about His will so you can choose if you want to do it [He does not operate that way!]. Pray! Think! But then, act! It does not matter which option you pick if it fits the parameters and is moving in the direction God calls us to go.

Don't worry about the details of how it is all going to happen. Many people allow their concerns to keep them from moving forward. Things like "How will I raise support?" or "How will I get the money for my dream?" become barriers. These are important issues. They do need proper attention. But trust God. He will work out the details. In Philippians 4:13, Paul says, "I can do all things through Christ who strengthens me." Paul wasn't saying, "I can do everything and anything I want." Rather, Paul is saying, "Whatever ministry God has called me to, I will be able to do, because it is God who will strengthen me to do it. I'm not dependent on others to allow me to do my ministry. I'm only dependent on God and He has promised He will give me the strength to do it." God knows you. He knows your future. He knows all the costs and the rewards of what He is calling you to do. And He already has worked out all the solutions to all the problems. Trust Him.

Now what? Get in step with God's direction. Pray hard. Think clearly. Listen well. Plan wisely. And get moving. You will be doing God's will!

No Matter What!

Though He slay me, yet will I trust in Him, and He also will be my salvation.
Job 13:15 KJV

Do you have the faith of Job? You can! Despite the loss of everything in this world we hold dear. Job kept his faith, he lost it all, his wife, children, health, friends, and wealth. But despite his misfortunes and what appeared to be total devastation, he moved his faith by the tiny mustard seed. He chose to use three words that changed his life. These three words will revolutionize YOUR faith. Although frequently manipulated by circumstances around them they are precise, purposeful, and powerful when it comes to growing your faith. Are you ready? Let's do it, trust God.......... NO MATTER WHAT!

When you are facing financial woes................Trust God NO MATTER WHAT!

When your friends and family abandon you......Trust God NO MATTER WHAT!

When your entire life is unraveling and seems to be tearing at the seams

Trust God NO MATTER WHAT!

Please share a time when it was difficult to trust God NO MATTER WHAT and Why?

_____

_____

_____

_____

_____

_____

_____

Whenever times get hard, and you don't know how you got wherever you are, let alone how you're going to make it out. Adapt one of my life's mottos: You must do what you can and God will do what you can't. This prayer reminds me of a prayer that symbolizes God's shadowing presence. This prayer is listed on the next page.:

FOOTPRINT'S PRAYER

I dreamed I was walking along the beach with the Lord, and
across the sky flashed scenes from my life.
For each scene I noticed two sets of footprints in the sand;
One belonged to me, and the other to the Lord.
When the last scene of my life flashed before us,
I looked back at the footprints in the sand.
I noticed that many times along the path of my life,
There was only one set of footprints.

I also noticed that it happened at the very lowest
and saddest times in my life
This really bothered me, and I questioned the Lord about it.
"Lord, you said that once I decided to follow you,
You would walk with me all the way;
But I have noticed that during the

most troublesome times in my life,
There is only one set of footprints.
I don't understand why in times when I
needed you the most, you should leave me.

The Lord replied, "My precious, precious
child. I love you, and I would never,
never leave you during your times of
trial and suffering.
When you saw only one set of footprints,
It was then that I carried you.

Conclusion

Remember in order to move your mustard seed, you must know God is with you. God is expecting us to be equipped for every good deed through Him. And, moving a mountain is a very thing He is expecting from us. Why? Because, He knows it can be done easily through faith in Him. Even with as little faith as a size of a mustard seed.

Endnotes

King James Version, Holy Bible

New International Version

Moved By A Mustard Seed~The Power Of Faith

Wonderfully Made FOUNDATION

Embrace ✤ Impart ✤ Empower

933 N.E. 32nd Street
Oklahoma City, OK 73105

www.thewonderfullymadefoundation.com

(405) 778-6870
wonderfullymadefoundation@yahoo.com

Connect with us:

TheWonderfullyMadeFoundation
WonderfullyMdF

Empowering Communities

Moved By A Mustard Seed~The Power Of Faith

Wonderfully Made Foundation

Wonderfully Made Foundation (WMF) is a 501c3 organization that was established in 2007 with programs and services that focus on personal development, life skills, domestic violence awareness, homeless assistance, and youth development and mentoring. WMF wishes to educate and promote empowerment holistically and empower individuals to succeed and live life to its fullest. Wonderfully Made Foundation also recognizes the needs of our youth and commits to empowering them with the tools to combat the disastrous effects of dating violence, low self-esteem, and peer pressure that often blinds their individuality and purpose. WMF provides a support system that will empower individuals to achieve.

Wonderfully Made Foundation Homeless Home

In August 2011, WMF opened the Wonderfully Made Homeless Home with goals to Embrace, Empower, and Impact the lives of individuals who are in need. The Home provides a 90 day transitional housing program to benefit women and children who are homeless. The Home offers a community area, a community kitchen, and a computer center. It also houses the Wonderfully Yours Clothing Closet and Toiletry Pantry for the less fortunate.

In addition to providing a place for families to call home, our organization also provides the following:
- Educational Opportunities such as GED classes and Job Readiness Training,
- Life Enrichment Classes (i.e. parenting, budgeting, credit repair, self-improvement, etc.),
- Case Management for Social Services, Housing Assistance, Counseling, and Bus Passes.

Wonderfully Yours Family Literacy Program

This program of the Wonderfully Made Foundation is designed to promote and enhance the literacy of everyone from early childhood to adulthood by providing books and activities to promote reading for the family.

Sweet Dreams

The Sweet Dreams program is a program designed to provide pajamas and a storybook to FIRST our homeless children and then ANY child in need in the metropolitan area!

Wonderfully Yours Clothing Closet

Wonderfully Yours provides:
FREE clothing, shoes, and toiletry items to ANY woman and child in need.

Other Programs:
- **Empowered Teens**
- **Empowered Magazine**

www.empoweredonlinemag.com

Made in the USA
Charleston, SC
26 March 2013